WISDOM WORDS

THE PATH

Words from the Shepperd of the Keeping

L. FRED BORDEN

authorHOUSE

AuthorHouse™
1663 Liberty Drive
Bloomington, IN 47403
www.authorhouse.com
Phone: 833-262-8899

Published by AuthorHouse   12/06/2022

ISBN: 978-1-6655-7635-2 (sc)
ISBN: 978-1-6655-7634-5 (e)

From the Shepperd
of the Keeping

Wisdom
Words

The Path

With Wailing Whistles
Wisdoms Words From
Within The Wells Wall.
Written With Keepers
Hand. A World Without
GODS Will Wrath Wasted.
We're Wise Watchtower
Watchers, Servant(s) Watching,
Waiting, Warning World.
Witnessing Willingly for JESUS.
AMEN

When Witness Weighs
What Warrior Writes Within.
Ways with woes wished wisely.

Intro

Welcome witness!
What is all this About?
Why are we Here?
What are we fearing? Why?
Well written wonders!
When "WILLED" with want.
Wrangled wise words.
Angels, Archangels
Invisible Spirit Beings
In a WORLD where?
When words won't work,
What will? Well!!
Without willingness we're
Wasting! Wise warnings,
Within watchtower windows,
willinglessly. 'Why?'
We're without wanting.
what we're witnessing!
'Witnessing what?'
What's wisely willed within,
what we wish.
'What wish?'
Wone with what we
would want!
'What's wanted?'
Word with watchtowers wide
watch. Words widened with
whelming width. Watchtowers
watchers. With words well
window whistled wildly!
With world weeping, while
we're well warmed with
wicked words wanting war.
Within wone world with

worsening weathers. What!
will we witness? When
we're well warned within
Wisdom Words written?
While witnessed with warriors
words written. Writings,
with working words written!
Well world! "whatsup?"
We're within wisdoms well.
Watch Wisely!
What words wished
will Well World within.
When?
Where?
Why?
With warnings wailing!!
What words will we want
"Whispered"?

Wone GOD!, wOne World,
wOne chance, wOne Heaven,
wOne people, wOne prayer,
wOne water, wOne air,
wOne Bible, wOne truth,
wOne word, wOne Will,
wOne Sun, wOne Moon,
wOne heard, wOne seen.
wOne wish, wOne giving.
wOne living, wOne life.
wOne blue sky, wOne time.
wOne Mother, wOne Father.
wOne Savior, wOne JESUS!

The Path

O'LO be thine names,
Pray with <u>thanks,</u>
ONLY AND ALWAYS
Finding: Wisdoms written
Plan, Direction and Path.
TO
OL'MIGHTY GOD
And his SON.
O'LORD JESUS our

<u>Christ</u> and <u>Savior</u>.
Now 718 Wisdom Passages as our
GOD WILLS TO WHOM HE CHOOSES,
AND SO LOVES THE WORLD.

1

While we watch wicked wishes, working wildy.

2

Words weaved, within world windows.

3

What we wish
will well, when
witnessed wisely.

———————

4

Wise wisdoms,
wished
world wide wildly.

5

Weakened wounds,
within
worlds will.

———————

6

Wonderful words,
whirling
world wonders.

7

Women will write, what world wash was, while witnessed.

8

Womens word, will waken world widely.

9

We wisely watch,
with wanting wish.

10

Watchtower words,
within worlds
wide windows,
watched

11

Wisdom words,
whirling
within world.

———————————

12

Wicked watchers,
wanting wreckage,
within wish.

13

Words without wisdom, wrapped with wickedness.

14

While we watch, wickedness wasting world.

15

White waters wrecking, whole wide world.

16

World wellness witnessed, with wisdom words.

17

Wellness wishes, within worlds windows.

18

World without wisdom writings, will waken weeping.

19

Words written
with warrior
works, within well.

———————

20

Watching while
wicked waste,
wells waters.

21

Wrangled W's
withold,
world wellness.

22

Walking within
wisdoms well,
with walls warning.

23

Wishings within
wells writings,
will wellnesses.

———————

24

World weepings
wrangling within
wicked weavers.

25

When wicked
weigh,
within wishes.

26

Within wisdoms
word wall, world
will witness wrath.

27

W's will work with
who's wellness wished,
worldwide wisely.

28

Without wickedness
world works,
work wonderfully.

29

Wells washing
with, wonderful
white waters.

30

Wisdoms words
will weave, what
world wishes.

31

Wellness wanted
worldly,
within wishes.

———————

32

Wise within wisdom
writes, what whoso
will want wished.

33

White water with whales, within wells.

34

Whosoever wisheth wisdoms wise, whensoever willed within wish.

35

Written wisdoms
write wise words,
within wells walls.

———————

36

Wisdoms wish,
with watchtower
wakened watchers.

37

Wicked wealth wrangled, without well wished wants.

38

We will witness with wicked waters, wwaves wreckage.

39

What we wish
when we want,
whosoever weeps.

———————

40

Wishingest wills
where wone walks,
when widely wrong.

41

Wicked willing, within wellness world.

42

Weighing world, while weed wanters watch.

43

When wickedest
world welledness,
wreck with waste.

44

Wrong wereships
will,
weaken watchers
will.

45

Wonderful words,

with

wonders whirling.

———————

46

While we wait

with wishers,

wanting weeds.

47

Wicked watching
without,
wellness wish.

———————

48

While weighing
with wishes,
world wants.

49

When watchers wait
while, wicked
waste waters.

50

Whosoever we
wish wellness with,
will well recieve.

51

Women will walk with willingness, within wisdoms.

52

Wholesomeness will wash world, with wise word.

53

With womens
wishednesses,
witnessed worldwide.

54

Watching while
wasted wisdom,
whithers wiseness.

55

With whatsoever
we wish,
when we wanted.

56

Working within
wisdom words,
without wait.

57

W's withold what world, wants within wereship.

58

With whatsoever we will want, when world weeps.

59

When wasting
weighs,
within world.

———————

60

Wright words
within,
wells wall witnessed.

61

Wisdom words,

within

wells walls.

———————

62

Wisely watching

with, wanting

wide wellnesses.

63

Watch women
will walk,
with wisdoms.

64

World wisdom
within,
womans wishes.

65

Weighing will, would well world.

66

Women will walk way without wastedness, whereverso wished.

67

Women will walk

wisely,

within wells words.

68

Wrecked wood

will, wrangle

worlds willingness

69

Wisdoms words wonderfully whirling, withinest worlds.

70

Waves wasting, without warning within waters.

71

Wisdoms words
whisper,
within well.

72

Wisdom words
washing world,
with wells wish.

73

With wakening
wide wisdoms,
within world.

───────────

74

Wise within
wishes,
wins wellness.

75

Without wishes,
wrongs
will wrangle.

―――――――

76

Wrangling wars
whistle within,
worlds windows.

77

Windows with
wicked words,
watched worldly.

78

Wicked watch,
without
world well wish.

79

When worlds
whisper,
within wise.

80

Wrangles with
what, we
want worldly.

81

Words without wise, won't work well.

82

When words, won't write, well wishes.

83

Whosoever wishes
wellness,
will wake wisely.

———————

84

Watching wicked
works, with
wrangling words.

85

Whoso wishes, what world whispers.

86

Wrangling words wegded, with world war.

L. Fred Borden

87

Wonderful wishes,
within womans
working wellness.

———————

88

Wonderful women,
working
within world.

89

Wonders working, with womens wow wish.

90

When watching wicked works, with weeping words.

91

Working willingly, without wickedness within.

———————————

92

When we wish within, whatsoever will work wellness.

93

Wealthy within wide worlds, wasting waters.

94

White waters with wales, wrecking wells.

95

Wealth within
world, with
wasted waters.

96

Wealth within
world,
wasting wellness.

97

Wicked words
won't whisper,
without wreckage.

————————

98

What words
would want,
wishes weighed?

99

What words
will we,
want written?

100

When waged
within wells,
wickened wishes.

101

When words,
want wishes
waged, wrangled.

102

When weeping
within whole
world, wrangles.

103

Wicked words,
would wegde
wanted wishes.

104

Women walking
well, within
weeping world.

105

What words, would want wishes waged?

106

Weeping world, without well wishes.

107

When women work
well, within
wasted world.

———————

108

Words wrangled
within wellnesses,
will well worlds.

109

Words wrangled
with wrong wise,
won't work well.

———————————

110

Whatsoever wants
within wickedness,
willed worldly.

111

When women
work well,
within weeping world.

112

Wickedness willed,
without wellness,
washes world.

113

Whatsoever with
whomsoever,
wills worldly.

114

Whatsoever wants
with wickedness,
willed worldly.

115

Watching women work with wise wishes, within world.

116

Watching worlds wellness wither, while we wish.

117

Watching wellness
wither,
with wickednesses.

———————

118

When we wish,
world
wellness within.

119

Warrior watches,

while world

wages wars.

———————

120

We want what,

worlds would

wish wisely.

121

Watching worlds withered wellness waste wayword.

122

Wereling worlds waged without wellnesses.

123

When we watch,
world wellness
wish wasting.

———————

124

Wise words written
worldwide, will
withold wellness.

125

Wells wall will weigh, what warrior witnesses.

126

Wild wrangling white waters, within wells.

127

Walking with
world wishes,
wanted wildly.

128

Washed with
wells water,
within world.

129

Woodill wood
will wrangle,
world willingness.

———————

130

Wonderful words,
whirling
world wonders.

L. Fred Borden

131

Wanting while waiting, with willingness.

132

While weighing weed wants, we'll wait.

133

Wisdoms words whirling, within wells.

134

Worldwide washing, with white waters.

135

When we want
wellnesses,
worldwide.

———————

136

We watch,
while wicked
waste world.

137

We watch, while
wicked
waste well water.

138

Wisdoms writings,
with words
wrangled wisely.

139

Wisdoms words with, whosoever wants wished.

———————

140

We want, what worlds would wish wisely.

141

We wereship what,
worlds would
wish wisely.

———————

142

When we wish
what we want
where we will.

143

Watching world
wellness,
wither wickedly.

———————

144

When we,
watch with
wickedness.

145

When we wish, within wickednesses.

146

World warriors, will work wellnesses wright.

147

Watchtower watch, will write wisdom words.

148

Waistline wereship within world windows.

149

Winfre wishes world wellness without wealth.

150

Will we wish wisely, when world wobbles?

151

Wisdom words,
will wrangle
with whoso wishes.

152

Water we want
within world,
will waste.

153

We watch wide
while, wicked
wealthy waste.

154

Why would
women worship
when wrong?

155

Wicked watch
without,
well wishes.

156

When we
want wellness
worldwide.

157

When will we,
want wellness,
worldwide?

———————

158

Well witnessed,
within what
wishes want.

159

Wealthy watch
worldwide
with wonder.

———————

160

Weighing weed
wishes,
while world waits.

161

Written words
within wisdom
well wished.

———————

162

Worldwide within
what, we're
well wishing.

163

What we worldly
well wishers,
want wished.

———————

164

Willingly waiting
without worry
within world.

165

World with wishes
wrangles
wise within.

166

With whosoever
wishes, wisdoms
will wrangle.

167

Written words
watched well
wisely work.

———————

168

Wisdom words
watched wisely
will win well.

169

Worlds with
wishes,
wrangle wisely.

———————————

170

Wisdom words
will wrangle
world windows.

171

Welcome wisdom
words with
whistling wows.

———————

172

Wonderful wish
with wellness
within world.

173

Wellness wishes wisely widely watched within.

174

What worldly well wishers want welled.

L. Fred Borden

175

Withering whole world weeping without waters.

176

World with, watchtower watch wasted.

177

When women
write what
washing was.

———————

178

Washing world
with
wright wereship.

179

Wrangling wealth
with weapons
wickedly willed.

———————

180

Words weighing
wisdoms will,
within w's.

181

Without words
we wonder
with wows.

———————

182

Without wise,
world wills
within wars.

183

What we want
within,
worlds wellness.

184

Whole world
willing within,
wellness wishes.

185

With wanting wish
we within world,
wisely watch.

———————————

186

Within what
we wish with,
when we want.

L. Fred Borden

187

Without waters within wells, world watches.

188

World with white waters, within wells.

189

Welcoming words, within wisdoms well walls written.

190

Wrangling word without will, wasting wellness.

191

What world
wants
within wisdom.

192

Weak watch
with what
world wishes.

193

When women walk with wisdoms words.

194

Worlds wone wisdoms written, with witness.

195

Watchtowers
words will well,
world wellness.

———————

196

When world
without well
water weeps.

197

World who
weeps without
wellness, whithers.

198

Wise wills
wisdoms, with
world well.

199

Wisdoms wall wrightings, with world wellness.

———————

200

With wone wish, what world wills within wellnesses.

201

Wrong waisted
wishes willed,
with wickedness.

———————

202

Warrior written
words, will well
wild whispers.

L. Fred Borden

203

Within world without wastes, washed white.

204

Wild winds with waves wrecking walls.

205

When world watches
without, wellnesses
withers with waste.

206

When wise willingly
wrangle, world
waste will weaken.

207

When windows whistle warnings weep.

208

Worst wrath witnessed within world windows.

209

Whipping woods within wild wicked winds.

210

Wider winds witholding wide whistling wreckage.

211

Watching wisdom
words with
wanting woes.

————————

212

Without wisdoms
we will wake,
wickedness within.

213

Wicked wishing
wreckage, within
worlds wells.

———————

214

Wrangling war
words with
wicked watchers.

215

Wrangling wicked wealthy, wanting world wasted.

———————

216

Wasted wellness watched within world windows.

217

Willings within
war, will waste
worlds wellnesses.

218

Weak weeping
wounded without
wells waters.

219

Watching worlds
well waters, waste
wither without wise
watchtowers word,
warnings written.

———————————

220

Wisdom wellness
working within world.

221

Waiting with want,
worlds well within
wellnesses wished.

———————

222

Wishes written,
within who's words
want wellness.

223

Wise words write,
when world will
wrangle with war.

———————

224

Wise words written,
with world watching
with wonder.

225

World without
wells waters
worldwide.

226

Worldwide white
water, washing with
wrecking waves.

227

Wicked watchers
will work wow
with witches.

———————

228

Weaving wickedness
within well wishes,
without want.

229

Wickedness will wipeout washedout world.

230

Wise word writings wishing wellness within womens want.

231

What's w's wish
with word well?

232

Witnessed when watched within world windows, with watchtower warnings written.

233

Whistled warnings
without watch
wavering wild.

234

Wisdoms wealthy,
weaving wishes
with wellness.

L. Fred Borden

235

Words wrangling wealth within, wished wickedness.

236

Whole world without wish wastes within.

237

Words wrangling
wealth
within wish.

238

Waking whole
world, with war
whistle warnings.

239

Wise words
will well world,
within wisdoms.

————————

240

Wisdom written
will wake world,
within wordship.

241

Wisdom worldwide without wild wickedness.

242

When women within world, wish wellnesses.

243

Wanting wish
with wealth
within windows.

244

Winning wealth,
with wishes,
without wicked.

245

Wanting wishes,
with
worldly wealth.

246

Wasted words
welcome,
wickeded ways.

L. Fred Borden

247

Wonderful waiting woman wishing wellness.

248

Wickedness wants world without women within.

249

Working well within what will work.

250

Washing with well waters within world.

L. Fred Borden

251

Wild wowes
with words
wanting war.

252

Winds wrecking
with white
water waves.

253

Worst winds world will witness wherever.

254

Ways with what world will wish.

L. Fred Borden

255

Whos wish within
what we want
will work within?

256

What world wishes,
with wars warning?
We wake with whistles,
wildly waleing!

257

Walls words
wash world
with wisdoms.

———————

258

Wicked want
world without
watchtower word.

259

Wisdom works within wise when willed.

260

Weeping world without well wishers wereship.

261

Waiting woman
watching while
wanting word,
with wone wanted.

———————

262

Wonderfully wowed
working woman,
waiting with wanting.

L. Fred Borden

263

Wild wereling white
waters washing world,
with wrecking wrath.

264

World weathers
will wip with wildly
wickened winds.

265

World wobble will
washout world, with
wrecking waves.

266

Working within
wisdom words, will
well world ways.

267

Welcome wisdom
words with what,
will work wellness.

———————

268

Wise watchtowers
willingness with
Wisdoms, will well
world wranglings.

269

What wisdom wants, will wow whole world.

270

When writings wrangle, wise wish within.

271

World will want
wellness within,
when wars wrangle.

―――――――――

272

Wakened world,
with wailed
whispers wrangled.

273

Watchers with
whistles waiting
world wide.

274

Without wakening
wrangling words
witling world war.

L. Fred Borden

275

When word will
welcome wars,
widely waged.

276

World with
wars wraths,
wrecking whatsoever.

277

Wicked wishers
wishing wreckage
with world war.

278

Wisdoms will wish
wellness without
wicked ways.

L. Fred Borden

279

Wisdoms will wish wellnesses, without wanting.

280

Within world where wicked wanters wereship.

281

Welling wished within worlds w5 word windows.

282

When written wisdoms, wrangle wise within world.

L. Fred Borden

283

Who wins where,
when with what
we watch wisely?

———————

284

Watchtowers
words written
with warnings.

285

When wishing without wellness within wanting.

286

Washed with wreckage, while world watches.

287

World with
wicked wishers
wanting wreckage.

———————

288

Warnings whispered,
within words
widely written.

289

World wobbles
wrangle wrecking
white waters.

290

Wisdoms word w's
wills wellnesses,
within whole world
when worked well.

291

Where wicked winds
with white waters,
whirling wreckage.

292

Wrecked world,
with wrangled
white waters.

293

With world
water wells,
witholding well.

294

Wishing within
what wellnesses,
will work widely.

295

World wastes, without wisdoms watchtower word.

———————

296

Wealthy wise women, wondering without want.

297

Wretchs walking
wonderlessly
within world,
wanting water
while we watch
with world window.

298

Wreckage with wretchs within whirling waves.

299

Wisdom words within wellness world, will work.

300

Wells wall will
wisely weigh, what
we witness when
world wobbles.
Without watchtower
warnings wailed,
within world windows.

L. Fred Borden

301

W warnings written with willing words, witnessed widely will well world. Without whistles wailing, when words waging wars waken with wrangle.

302

With wisdom words
written, worlds
wishes witnessed.

303

Within washedout
well, writes what
world will witness,
without wakening.

304

Waken world,
with wonderful
wise wisdoms.

———————

305

We won't win with,
what white water
will wreck widely.

306

Wells wall will
weigh worth, with
what wisdoms
warrior writes.
While witnessing
when world wrath,
will waste westward.

L. Fred Borden

307

Wise watcher,
warns without
wicked wish.

308

Weeping wows,
whispered with
wretched word.

309

Wealthiest wallets
working within,
wicked wantings.

310

Warrant welcoming
when wisdoms,
waken worldwide.

L. Fred Borden

311

Warmths worth
weighed, within
weather windows.

———————

312

Whistling winds
wakening world,
with wild wreckage.

313

Worst wealthy
working, within
worsening winds.

———————

314

Wreckage within
weather waves,
will wrangle world-
wide worry.

315

Wisdoms warn
with word walls,
widely welling world.

316

Weeping willows
wailer, will write
wisdoms witnessed.

317

Wisdoms warn
within wellings,
when wereshipped.

———————

318

War wasted
world, with
weeping widows.

319

World wills
wealth within
wants, when wished.

———————

320

Wealth within
worlds, wettined
wells waiting.

321

We want,
we wish,
we won't.

322

Within why
wone wishes,
without way.

323

Wedging with,
wedding warmly
wished well.

———————

324

What's wished
when we,
want wealth.

325

Waters with
winter, will
worsen west.

326

Weather with
wrecking winds,
wrangling worldwide.

L. Fred Borden

327

Watch words, with wise witnessing.

328

Wone word, with what was willed.

329

Wone word
with what,
was wished.

330

Written within
wone word,
where we wonder.

L. Fred Borden

331

World was
word wished,
with wone will.

———————

332

World was
wone word,
within wishings.

333

Weeping wounded
world, wasting
without wisers.

334

Wone windows
wiser, will waken
with wisdom words.

L. Fred Borden

335

Wone wish
within world,
was wasted.

———————

336

When winds
whistle, with
wone word.

337

Wone wound within world, wills wrath.

338

Wishes within wrecking winds, without warning.

L. Fred Borden

339

Why? would we,
write with words
waging wars?

———————————

340

Weakness with
wickedness, will
wrangle wastes.

341

Wasted world,
within what
wickened want.

342

Wone world,
with wone
will wanted.

Without what's
written, worlds
wellness will
wrinkle. While
we wounder why
world weighs,
what we wish.

344

Wills within when
what was wished,
when we went wacked
with wicked war
wishers, wanting
world wasted
with wealthiest.

L. Fred Borden

Waste within
water wells
warning, won't
wake world wide
without worries,
watched within
worlds windows.

346

Wars will waste
well waterholes,
while we work
with wickedness.

347

Winds whistle
wild warnings.

L. Fred Borden

Words written
with wordsmith
were well willed,
while world was
wakened, with
watchtowers wise
watching wildness.

349

Wone world, with wone wanted wish.

350

Wakening world, with words written well.

L. Fred Borden

351

Windows wailing word whistles, with wars will.

352

Watch when wone word. wastes wellness,

353

Wishes without
wise with wisdom
won't, welcome
what's wanted
when we're
within wereship.

354

Walking with
wisdoms when
we wish, wants
within what
world will weigh
with wellness.

355

Wealth wellers
wereship, with
wicked worth.
wanting wrath,
with wreckaging
worldwide waste.

356

Wise work with
worlds wastes,
will welcome wellness.

357

Wallowing with
words, wisdom
wants working.

358

Wicked willing
weakened world,
without wellness.

———————

359

<u>God</u> willed water
worlds wellnesses,
with wone wish.

360

Wailed wisdoms
warn world,
when written.

———————

361

Words write
what was
willed within.

362

Wisely watch, water
wells, witholding
weathered wastes.

363

Welcome with wise,
what wisdoms
wish within world.

364

Witches wond,
working within
worsening winds.

365

Wickeded work
with worlds wealth,
wrangling wreckage.

366

Willing with wone wish, within wanting.

———————

367

Wisemans word writings, within wantings worked.

368

Waiting within
windows watching
weird weather.
wrecking world
with wildly
wicked winds.

369

Watching without
willingness, was
what we worked
within, while we
witnessed warnings.

———————————

370

Wone world witnessing.

371

Wishings with
wone world,
wasted wickedly.

———————

372

Wrangling waste
will win, without
wise wisdoms.

373

What was willed, was with wone.

374

Wone word willed world.

375

When world wallop, weakens watchers.

376

When whole world
will want wone
wish willed. with
wasteful weapons
wrath wreckage.
wheresoever we've
witnessed within.

377

Wasted wealth
with weapons,
will wreck
western world.

378

With wone
world wasted.

L. Fred Borden

379

Wealthiest with
weapons, want
wone world.

———————

380

Wisers working
wickeded words,
within watch.

381

Watchtower words,
written with
wise wakening.

382

Wakening world,
with wisdoms
wise warnings.

L. Fred Borden

383

Welcoming world
with widest wish,
when what wasn't
with world, when
willed with wone
without wicked.

384

Welcome wise
witness, we're
wone withour
world while
we, wish within
when we're welled
with wisdom words.

385

Walking without worried wantings.

386

Wone word won't will, what we've wished with.

387

Wealthiest willingly
want, welling with
watchtower word.

388

Water within
world wells,
will wipe way
with wastage.

L. Fred Borden

389

Warmed world
without, winters
windy weathers.

———————

390

Worlds worse
winds, within
winter weather.

391

Wise words
wishing widened
wellnesses within.

392

Wall writings
with wisdom,
well written.

L. Fred Borden

393

Watch wicked
weather worsen,
without warning.

————————

394

Wise willings
with warnings,
written within.

395

Wicked wealthy, worsening winds within weather.

396

Warming world, will wrangle white wrecking waters.

397

Walls writings written without wellness within world watcher windows, wailing wasting words willingly wickeded.

398

Wealthy wrangled
within worlds
wells, waiting
with wickeded
wishes, wanting
world wasted
with wreckage.

399

While world
wobbles we
will wail, with
weeping want.

400

With wone
wrecking wind
wailing wrath.

401

Wishing wones with wickedness, welcomes wrath.

402

Wisdoms with wellness, work well within.

L. Fred Borden

403

Waves will wash waters within wells.

404

When watch weakens, world wills within wickednesses.

405

Welcomed wicked,
without watcher
warning whistles.

———————————

406

Work writings
with, wone
wise wereshipper.

L. Fred Borden

407

Willed works
with, wisdoms
words written.

408

Waken with
what, wisdoms
would want,
within world.

409

Warning won't, waken world within, while wobbles wrangle.

410

Watchout, with wise willingness, when weerie.

411

Wakened witness,

with wise words,

written within.

———————————

412

Wise woman,

welling wishes,

with wordboard

writings.

413

Wrangled wakenings,
welling world,
within watch.

———————

414

Windows wealth,
wrangled with,
wicked wish
witnessed.

415

Walls with,
wicked words,
written within.

416

Wisdoms will,
wish wellnesses,
within word.

417

Wisdoms within,
wickedness wished,
will wrecken.

———————

418

When weakening
within wone,
whole wide
world warned.

419

Where we wish,
with what we
witness, when
we're wanting.

———————

420

Wone wereshipper,
without wrangle,
working wisdoms.

421

World will willingly
welcome, warriors
written words.

_____

422

Without wicked
wants wasted
with wraths.

423

Wealthy wicked
women, wondering
world wide.

424

Wisdoms within
wickedness wish,
well witnessed
with watchtower.

Wisdom Words

425

Warning well written within.

_____

426

When wasting watchers warning

_____

427

Whole world warned wonce.

428

Will within
won't, weigh
well, with world.

———————

429

Wrecked world,
with what, we
will witness.

430

Wrangling white
waters, without
watcher warning.

431

Wicked waves,
with weight,
wrecking worlds.

432

Wreckage within,
without waters,
wearing ways.

———————

433

Weighing wone,
worlds worth,
with wickedness.

434

Weight with wones, wishes with wereship.

435

Wrecked world, with wrangled white waters.

436

Who will win?,
while we waste
worlds wealth,
with weapons.

437

Weapon within
waters, workup
white waves.

438

Who will win?
without wisdoms
within wereship

___

439

Who will win?,
with world wars
wreckaging wrath.

___

450

Wone wins world

451

When wereship,
weighs worthless,
within word.

452

Wone word
weighs, with
wide, worldly
wonderfulness.

453

When waiting
with what,
word writes.

———————

454

Working within
wrong wereships
we're wasting
wellness wishings

455

Which women,
will walk with,
wisdom words?

456

Wise women
working, with
wakenings, we
will witness.

457

Words wanting,
whispered with
wright wones.

458

Wone wish
within whole,
wide world
wanting wellness.

L. Fred Borden

459

Without wasting
wealth, within
wanted weapons.

460

Wonderful world,
without wicked,
wishes within.

461

Without weapons, worlds won't, wage wars.

———————

462

World watches work, with wicked ways.

L. Fred Borden

463

Will within
what was,
was witled,
with wone,
wanted wish.

———————

464

When we're with,
wonderful whisper.

465

Which ways will we walk, when world wobbles, with wrath?

466

World will, wonder why, with weather.

467

Wone wish within.

468

Wellness without waste.

469

Whole world wanting.

470

Wealth without wicked.

471

What world wants,
with wone wereship.

472

Watching when,
we're, witness
with wone.

473

Wanting, when
we wish with,
wickened will.

L. Fred Borden

474

Wereship with wone wrong word written

_____

475

Winning what? when we're without wisdoms

476

Witness while, worldwide weather watch, worsens.

477

Wicked weather warning, within windows word.

L. Fred Borden

478

World works
within wone,
willed wish.

479

Want with
wish, we
work within.

480

Without watch, we're without, welled warning.

481

When without wake, we will wait.

L. Fred Borden

482

Weather watcher, wild wheeling, with winds.

483

Weaving wishes, within wanted wickednesses.

484

Work with wone worldly woman, witholding wiseness

485

Wise women wanting wone world wish.

486

Wars words whistle, world-wide, within watchtowers.

487

Why would we want warnings well whistled?

488

Willing what
wishes, wish
when willed.

489

World winds
worsen, with
wrangling wicked
wreckage.

490

While watcher
warnings, wimper
words wasted.

———————

491

Winey wicked
weakly women,
weeping wow
with watch.

492

W's within wise words written, widely witnessed.

493

Winters wrath waves, without warming weather.

L. Fred Borden

494

With weathers worsened winds, we will weaken.

495

Wicked won't want wellness, within world-wide window.

496

World witnessing
with, well wisdom
writings willed.

―――――――

497

World wisdom
words wisely
written wright.

498

Wishes worldwide,
wanting wellness,
without wickednesses.

499

We will wish
wickedness,
willinglessly,
without will.

500

We!, with what world would want, will worry.

501

Warning world without, whistles wailed.

502

With wailing
whistles, word
wisdoms written.

503

Wwaves with
wicked watchers,
weighing wreckage.

504

When wicked will wreck, world within well.

505

Wone welled world, without wicked way.

506

When we're wanting what's willed with wone.

507

Without waste within, will widen welcome welling.

508

Windows working
with, wicked
wishing wealthy.

509

Watch windows
words, with
wiseness wakened.

L. Fred Borden

510

Window with
worse, wicked
works within

511

Working ways,
without watch,
within wellness.

512

W's within world
windows, working
witchunt watch.

513

Weather watchtower
warrior, witnessing
within wreckage.

514

Wanting wishes with wild wicked worldly wealth

515

Wicked wealthy with, wrangled war weapons, waiting.

516

With what we watch, we're widely warned.

517

Wellness wrangled with waste, without word warnings.

L. Fred Borden

518

Wants with,
wone word
written, work.

519

Wakened wise
works, with
wones willness.

520

Wealth with wisdoms word, work wellness.

521

Window will, warn world, without whistle.

L. Fred Borden

522

Waken with, world wisdom words written.

523

Without words, we will watch, world waste.

524

While wisdoms
waken with
words willed

525

Wright words
written within
world witness

526

Wise work will waken world with words wrangled

———————

527

Wone womans words, when weather worsens.

528

Wicked without
weapons, will
wrong world,
with wastedness.

529

Watchtower words
within watch
windows waiverd

530

When woman
warns, watch
what we will
witness, with
worsening,
weather.

531

Working within
world, with
wild weather.

————————

532

Waiting while
watching, weather
worsen wickedly.

533

What words
will waken
world widely

———

534

Wise wakening,
will wrangle
world, with
wone word.

535

Wealth within world wellness, works well.

536

When will wise words work wantingly with witholding?

537

Within where,
words work,
will withold.

538

Windows warn,
with wicked
words wailed.

539

Worlds worsening
weather, within
wells, without
watchtowers wide
window whistle.

540

Wone willed wish!!
with warrior word.

L. Fred Borden

541

When women,
walk within
wone world,
without war
weapon worry,
when we waken,
with willingness.

542

Watching wone
walk, with
wanting wish.

———————

543

Waiting with
wone, wish
witheld within.

L. Fred Borden

544

While waiting
without wells,
wishes won't
work with
what, we're
wanting within
widely wished.

545

Women willing
without, wicked
wish welcomed.

———————

546

Wanting wone
world, wellness
wisely wished.

L. Fred Borden

547

Who wishes
with women!
what we want?

548

Wone woman
with, words
warning world.

549

Warning within womans words with weather worsening while we're watching

550

Wone warning,
with wone
woman, wrangling
watchtowers
worldwide, within
windows watch.

551

Weather worsening, without warnings, within windows.

552

Wake with what will well world.

553

When we watch,
woman warn,
with worsening
weather warnings.

554

Within wicked
worsening weather,
wrangling worldly.

555

Wone world,
with women,
working with,
wone world,
wellness wish.

———————

556

Woman warning
within windows.

L. Fred Borden

557

Wings with
wheels watch
world well.

———————

558

Wow! what a
world we're
wreckaging!

559

Wellness wishes within weather watchtowers!

560

Why would? we!, want world weather, worsening without watch?

561

Wicked wanting
weather watch,
without window
warning.

———————

563

Worried watchers
wondering, what will
weather wrangle?

564

Wicked wanting
weather watches
without windows

565

Welcoming wise
watch words with
written warning
wellnesses.

566

Wasted words
with wicked
wealthy wishes.

567

Walls words
wrangled
wone way!

568

War with white
waters wrecking
world without
watchers warning

569

Who's with
wrangled words
written.

L. Fred Borden

570

Wone way we're wrong with world wars words.

———————

571

Within wone wanting without wickednesses.

572

Witholding well wantings within wone world.

573

Why will wone world word work wounders?

574

Why would wone world word work?

575

What with! would wisdoms work wrangled?

576

With what wish, would we will?

577

Who wishes wicked, wanted within willing.

578

Where we're
wicked, won't
well willingly.

579

Wicked wrangle
with words
widely weaved.

580

Well written
wickedness within
wone woven word.

581

Wone with world
will win wellnesses
wildly willinglessly.

L. Fred Borden

582

Welcomely without wise watch we wish well want.

583

Walking within wicked words, will welcome wide wreckage.

584

Words within
worlds wicked
wall, welcome
wars worldwide.

585

We're wone world
walking within
wicked wantings.

586

Wasting works,
worldly without,
wise watchtower.

587

Walking with
what will
welcome wellness.

588

World without watch women wanting wellness

589

Without worldly word we will wither.

L. Fred Borden

590

Wasting works
worldly with
watchtower.

591

With waste
we wanted
wone wish.

592

Wisdoms work within wellnesses wishing.

593

Witholding well waters will waste worlds.

L. Fred Borden

594

Witholding well wishes within wones wish.

595

World watches war wranglers wrecking.

596

Witholding wone wicked wish wanted within.

597

Waking with war wrangle walking.

L. Fred Borden

598

World with
windows wasting
weather word

_____

599

With world
windows wrangling
wickedness.

600

We wisely watch with wanting wellnesses.

601

Wisdom words we want within world.

L. Fred Borden

602

Watchtower
world within
wisdom writings.

———————

603

Wrangled wicked
wealth with
wellness wish.

604

We wisely
watch with
wanting wishes.

605

Wasted well
waters, within
war weaponry.

606

Werely weakened world, without wise watch.

———————

607

Werey weak world without well waters.

608

Wasted weakness without wanting wellness.

609

World without wicked wasting weapons.

L. Fred Borden

610

With war weapons wasting well waters.

611

Wicked weakness witholding wish without wellness.

612

Wicked wealthy warmongers wasting wealth.

613

Wars wwaves will wreck worlds works.

L. Fred Borden

614

Wild white
waters wrecking
works within.

———————

615

When wisdoms
word wants
wellness willed.

616

What! wisdom writing will we! want wished?

617

We will, we wish, we want.

L. Fred Borden

618

We want welded wisdoms working within.

619

Well wished wiseness, wills wisdoms wished.

620

Welding wisdoms
within world
will waken wiseness.

———————

621

Watchers with
wone wish we
will want worldly

622

Wellness wanting without weakness well wasted.

623

We will want wicked wishes with wants.

624

Wise watching
wills wone
wisdom wish.

625

Willing without
wickedness will,
will welledness.

L. Fred Borden

626

With what witness will we wish with?

———————

627

Wisdoms written with wone wish, witheld within wone world.

628

Winds without wellness wrecks without warning.

629

Written words within wisdoms well wished.

L. Fred Borden

630

What world wishes with war waged?

631

Why we wish wicked wantings.

632

While wishes wegded with words wobbled.

633

Wisdoms wish will wegde wanted withdrawl.

L. Fred Borden

634

Washing weakness
with well waters

635

Will withdraw
weather world
wars wishes

636

What will
wickedness wither?

637

Wills wearing wealth, wound with windows.

638

What will we witness within world wars?

639

Wells walls
will weigh
what wisdoms
warrior writes.

———————

640

With wisdom
words written.

641

We will

win with

what waters

want washed.

_____

642

World well

wishes witnessed.

L. Fred Borden

643

What will world watch when war wages.

——————————

644

We will well wish when watching.

645

When we witness worlds wraths.

646

Watching wisely, will work with winners.

L. Fred Borden

647

Will wicked win with wars waged?

648

What will wicked ways win?

649

When wars wegded with weakness, wreck

650

World will wither with wasted waters

L. Fred Borden

651

When willing
with wone
wishing want

652

Waiting within
watchtower
walls watching

653

When we
will what
wicked want

654

Wondering why
waiting works
well within?

L. Fred Borden

655

Who weighs
what we
want
When we wish?

———————

656

Without will
wicked win
wasted world

657

While waiting
we wish
with wellness

658

Wailing wall
within worlds
wisdom well

L. Fred Borden

659

Withdrawl with
wickeded wish
washed white

660

We will witness,
wone wrecking
white water
world.

661

When we will wish with wellnesses.

662

Within wellness wish, with what we want.

L. Fred Borden

663

Waters without
will, wrecking
wooden walls.

———————

664

While we
watch wicked
wishes, working.

665

Wealth will wither world without watchers.

666

Wicked watch while world war, wishes widens.

L. Fred Borden

667

While widows
watch without,
warmths weeping.

———————————

668

Well wishing
will work
wonders.

669

Wise words
will wither
wicked wishes.

670

Words will
waken wide
wellness within.

671

Work will
waken what
watchers want.

———————

672

Work will
waken wide
wellness withol.

673

What will!
wishes will?

674

Well wishes
without wickedness.

675

Waiting with
willingness.

L. Fred Borden

676

Women wait, while world withers way.

_____

677

While world wrangles with wrong words.

678

Women wait, while world wrangles within wrong.

679

We wish, within when wanted.

L. Fred Borden

680

Wicked wages
will weaken
world writes.

681

Wedging wirthy
words without
wickedness.

682

Within what world will words work?

683

When well wishes will work.

684

When will
wishes will,
work?

685

Walking with
wisdom will
work well!

686

Wanted wicked
ways, with word
willing wishes.

———————

687

Wanting wellness,
with words
well wished.

L. Fred Borden

688

Watching with
wedged wakeness,
within window

———————

689

Wise wonder,
within wisdoms
wailing wall.

690

What wellnessers want wicked within wishes?

691

Watching with wedged wakeness

692

Without waters, world will waste.

L. Fred Borden

693

Waged wakenings with world war, will waste worlds.

694

Wise words within wisdoms well, will work.

695

Without wise wisdom, will withdraw words.

696

Worldly warnings within waters wrangling waves.

697

Wise weighs wisdom, when wanting.

698

With wisdom wrong will write within.

699

Women without wisdom, will write wrong.

700

With wishes, world wars waged wickedly.

701

While we
wedge wish
with wisdom.

———————

702

Wars wittled,
with wealths
wickedness wished.

703

When worlds
wish war
within wickedness.

704

Water within
world will
wash wickedness.

L. Fred Borden

705

Will warnings
withdraw!
wicked wishes?

―――――――

706

What will
work, with
wickedness
wantings?

707

Women with weakness withdraw while world watches.

708

Working with world wasting wishers.

L. Fred Borden

709

When wicked
withdraw, world
will win wellness.

710

Written warnings
will wake
world widely.

711

Work within
warrior words,
without waste.

———————

712

Work with wise
words warrior
writes.

713

With weakness, we will wither weepingly.

714

Write with wise words wisely, with willingness.

715

When wished wellness, works within world.

716

Working with world wars wounded, wisely.

717

Walls with warnings, well written wisely.

718

Well witnesses! what wickedness will withold world wellness? "Aluf"

Isaiah
Seventh <u>seal</u>
for Shepard
77777777

Found
2017

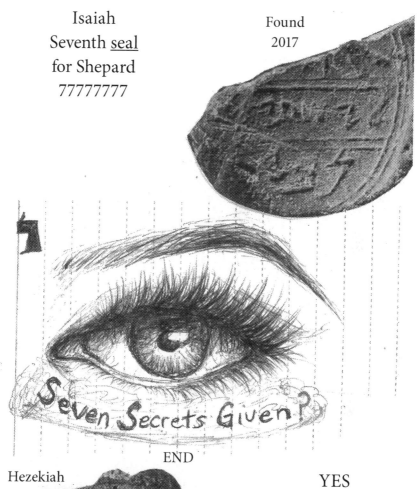

Seven Secrets Given?

END

Hezekiah

2017
Found

YES
THE WORDS OF
JESUS
BAHA'I

<u>Marker</u>
for Jewel
To the PATH